# YO' MAMA!

# YO' MAMA!

## BUST-O-PEDIA

### Snap C. Pop and Kid Rank

BERKLEY BOOKS, NEW YORK

# YO' MAMA!

A Berkley Book published by arrangement
with the authors

PRINTING HISTORY
Berkley trade paperback edition/May 1995

ISBN: 0-425-14861-0

BERKLEY®
Berkley Books are published by The Berkley Publishing Group,
200 Madison Avenue, New York, New York 10016.
BERKLEY and the "B" design
are trademarks belonging to Berkley Publishing Corporation.

PRINTED IN THE UNITED STATES OF AMERICA
10   9   8   7   6   5   4   3   2   1

To my mom, my sister and Steve O. for all their love and support.
—Kid Rank
To my agent and editor (Yo'office is so messy . . .), Dar Dar,
Sandra L., Dammit Janet, Maxey Pad, Susie Q., Sandy Beaches,
my mama (sorry, Dad), Doc. Stevo and the crew, Mikey Boy, Christ R.,
and Joe. Joe who? Joe mama!
—Snap C. Pop

Thanks to all mamas the world over, plus a few mamas
we thought deserved **special** mention . . .

. . . Hillary Clinton—"the big mama on the **hill**"

. . . Roseanne—for making it **easy** for us to come up
with all the jokes in the first chapter

. . . Oprah, who, bless her heart, avoided being in this book by changing
from fat to skinny, skinny to **fat, fat** to skinny (we gave up)

. . . The Little Old Lady who lived in a shoe, had so many children . . .
What—you never **heard** of birth control, you slut?

# YO, 'TSUP?

MAMAMAMAMAMAMAMAMAMA**viii**MAMAMAMAMAMAMAMA-

and women were sold as property and forced to endure gross civil and ethical injustices. Some fared better than others in this struggle to survive, but perhaps the most difficult hardships were endured by those black men who had some type of handicap and couldn't exact a price of much worth on the slave market.

These "inadequate" or "damaged" slaves were packaged in groups of twelve and sold that way at bargain basement rates to anyone who would have them. Being one of the twelve in a group of "Dozens," as they were called in those days, was considered to be the ultimate insult by the black community at large . . . and the ultimate horror. Members of the Dozens were forbidden to speak out to their "owners" about the harsh and often inhumane conditions in which they were forced to live, and fighting amongst themselves was considered a severe crime punishable by flogging and even death in some cases.

Under this extreme oppression, a relatively safe outlet emerged for venting fear, frustration, and anger that wouldn't result in punishment. Known as the "Game of Dozens," this challenge was a game of power not measured by physical strength, but by words and wit, in which players engaged in insulting banter to determine a victor. Besides serving as a pressure valve, the Game of Dozens also gave the black slave communities a way to set and maintain a hierarchy of dominance and leadership under restrictive circumstances.

Playing the Dozens was always done in front of a crowd, since it was a battle for dominance; playing it without an audience was worthless, except for practice. With peers as judges, the mouth was truly mightier than the sword—two opponents sparring against one another to a cheering crowd, delivering blow after blow of insults. Back and forth, Dozens battles would rage until one patriarch stood the victor and unwritten leader of the Dozens group.

While the topic of a Game of Dozens could be anything and everything—from facial features to bad breath—the most powerful insults began with the phrase "Yo' Mama." This was in large part because the mother in black society held an esteemed position and the duty and role of the son was one of protection borne of admiration and love. Given that sons were often separated from their mothers in those days, sold off to other plantations or enclaves, memories of Mama were considered to be precious and mamas became the subjects of the ultimate insults. Because Dozens aimed at Mama had the most impact, they became the most widely used. Once Mama was mentioned in a Game of Dozens, there was no going back—they were all going to include "Yo' Mama's" from then on. And so, "Yo' Mama" insults were born and fast became the focus of playing and winning the Game of Dozens.

In the days of slavery and beyond, Dozens survived by being passed down from generation to generation as a social ritual. A hundred years later, the Game of Dozens has become mainstream among African-Americans and other populations, popularized on the streets and in the media. A popular TV show, *In Living Color*, hosts a *Jeopardy!*-type version of the Game of Dozens called "The Dirty Dozens" where contestants pick Dozens categories such as "Fat," "Stupid," etc., and battle it out with the best Yo' Mama insults. And although few viewers know the game's true roots and history, it still serves much of the same purpose to African-Americans and, increasingly, to the general populace at large, both to release tension and settle conflicts without violence, and to help establish a pecking order or social hierarchy among groups.

One thing has changed, however, and that's the name by which the Game of Dozens is known. Today, the Dozens goes by many aliases—Ranking, Snapping, Busting, Capping, and Slamming to name a few—and the playing rules vary quite a bit from hood to hood. In this book, we're going to show you all the different ways people play the Dozens and the rules by which they play, plus we'll introduce to you the "official YMB" rules of the game, to set a standard, so to speak.

We'll also give you Yo' Mama busts from the streets of America that you can use in battle, and methods to come up with your own. Before you know it, you'll be slammin' yo' opponents and be ready for a challenge at any time. At the end of the book, you can even send us some of your original Yo' Mamas by filling out the form in the "Yo! We'll Make You Famous!" chapter. If we use yours in our next book, *Mo' o' Yo' Mama*, we'll put your name by your insult and you'll go down in history. We'll send a copy of the book for each of the first 100 busts we receive and choose, so send in yours today! Thanks.

# OFFICIAL RULES

## INTRODUCTION

The Game of Dozens, like other games that have grown up on the street, have taken on some universal "unwritten" rules by which most players abide (e.g., there must be an audience; no physical contact allowed; always nonviolent). But there has never been a set of "official" rules of play that people can fall back on when there's a dispute—no way of scoring like a boxing match. We thought that it was time to change that.

The Official YMB (Yo' Mama Bust-O-Pedia) Dozens rules incorporate many of the unwritten rules of the street that have been adopted over time, in addition to offering some ideas for organized challenges, a way of scoring for advanced players, and guidelines to go by, if you choose to use them. From now on, if there's a dispute, you'll have a reference to consult to settle it.

## BEFORE YOU BEGIN

Choose an emcee or referee who will set the rules (choosing from the options that follow) or restate the rules to the crowd before the match as requested by the opponents. The emcee will also watch for fouls and other calls and may play the role of judge and executioner, crowd mediator (this is a democracy), or scorekeeper if the YMB scoring system is used. It's not all work though; this is a time for an emcee to turn on the juice. He or she could even start with something like, "Ladies and gentlemen, we bring to you . . . In this corner [on this sidewalk, etc.], weighing in at . . . the champion . . . in this corner . . ." etc.

## TYPES OF DOZENS GAMES

There are two ways a Dozens match can be run:

1) *Street Fight:* No set rounds or time limits. The loser eventually forfeits. These battles can be won in a matter of seconds or last for more than an hour, depending upon how evenly matched and resourceful the opponents.

2) *Three Round Competition:* Three rounds; 5 minutes of battle per round. Variation could be less or more (e.g., 2 minutes; 10 minutes) per round. First opponent to win two rounds wins this competition (i.e., if someone wins first two rounds, the game is won). This type of competition requires an emcee or referee who starts the rounds, stops them, and gets the reaction from the crowd.

## COMMON CHALLENGES

There are three common types of Dozens challenges. They can be played as either a Street Fight or with the Three-Round Competition format, with or without scoring:

1) *One-on-One Challenge:* Most common challenge between two adversaries.

2) *Buddy Challenge:* Teams of two compete with one another, taking turns delivering busts.

3) *Tag-Team Challenge:* Usually teams of two against two, where each team is allowed four tag-offs for a one-round Street Fight or two tag-offs per five minute round (for an official Three-Round Competition).

## SPECIAL CHALLENGES

There are two other special challenges with different rules for rounds and timing, and you can make up your own versions of these or invent your own:

1) *Speed Dozens:* Each individual or team has fifteen seconds to complete a bust. Game lasts for 10–15 minutes (40 to 60 busts per game). If either opponent or team goes over the 15-second limit more than three times in that game, it automatically forfeits. Therefore normal "Delay of Game" penalties do not apply here.

2) *Family Feud–Type Challenge:* Two teams of four or five battle it out with an emcee who gives out topics in 10 short rounds, and players give busts on topics in round robin fashion from one team to another.

## OFFICIAL RULES

## ISSUING A CHALLENGE

There are two ways you can issue a challenge:

1) *Spontaneously Challenge:* These can happen anywhere and they do. No advance planning, just the challenge.

2) *Duel Challenge:* For the more romantic at heart, a healthy bout of Yo' Mama at sundown adds to the excitement of the fight. This is the I'll-see-you-on-the-playground-after-school type of challenge.

## BEGINNING THE GAME

The emcee begins by announcing the challenge. The contest begins officially with the first Yo' Mama blow.

## OFFICIAL RULES

## SCORING & WINNING

Opponents can win either by:

*Popular Vote:* In which spectators cheer or vote for the winner of each round. Whoever gets the loudest cheers wins. If it's a Three-Round bout, the crowd votes at least two times and a third time if the first two rounds were a tie.

*Scored Vote:* Similar to how it's done in boxing. Like a boxing match, if an opponent leaves the ring at any time (walks away from the challenge), he or she forfeits the game and the other opponent wins by TKO (Technical Knockout). If a match is really important and you want to score it fairly, pick one to three people (or even the whole audience if you want, but that can get a little hard to manage with a big crowd) and use the following guidelines to score that match.

Here's the official Yo' Mama Bust-O-Score system:

| EVENT | POINTS |
|---|---|
| Great Bust | 3 |
| Good Bust | 2 |
| Fair Bust | 1 |
| Poor Bust | 0 |
| Already Used Bust | -1 |
| Delay of Game (more than 30 seconds) | -2 |
| Physical Contact (minor foul) | -5 |
| Violent Physical Contact (illegal foul) | Forfeit |

Obviously, whoever has the most points at the end—except if there's a forfeit or TKO—wins. When forfeits and TKOs happen, it's common to see rematches on another day when the opponent's wits are sharper.

# OFFICIAL RULES

## TIME-OUTS

Players may elect to also have one, two, or three optional one-minute time-outs for each team in a game to get their bearings. Or each opponent or team could be given one 30-second time-out per round for each round. The emcee/referee decides this.

# APPEARANCE

**Yo' Mama's so fat . . .**
she sells shade.

**Yo' Mama's so fat,**
they have to airlift her out of bed every morning.

**Yo' Mama's so fat,**
when she runs, she looks like a buffalo in heat.

## YO' MAMA'S SO FAT . . .

**Yo' Mama's so fat,**
when she sits around the house, she REALLY
sits around the house.

**Yo' Mama's so fat,**
her clothes have stretch marks.

**Yo' Mama's so fat,**
she buys group insurance.

**Yo' Mama's so fat,**
instead of Levis 501 jeans, she wears 1002s.

### Yo' Mama's so fat,
when she walks through Los Angeles, she registers a 7.2 on the Richter Scale.

### Yo' Mama's so fat,
even Arsenio couldn't kiss all her butt.

### Yo' Mama's so fat,
she has her own area code.

### Yo' Mama's so fat,
when she wears a red dress, everyone yells, "Hey Kool-Aid!"

**Yo' Mama's so fat,**
whenever she goes swimming in the ocean, baby whales can be seen nursing on her breasts.

**Yo' Mama's so fat,**
when she dances the band skips.

**Yo' Mama's**
on a seafood diet: when she sees food, she eats it.

**Yo' Mama's so fat,**
if she bent over, they could show two movies on her butt.

**Yo' Mama's so fat,**
she has to iron her clothes in a parking lot.

**Yo' Mama's so fat,**
she doesn't walk, she rolls.

**Yo' Mama's so fat,**
she uses a hula hoop as a pinkie ring.

**Yo' Mama's so fat,**
she uses a mattress for a Kotex.

**Yo' Mama's so fat,**
all her clothes have to be custom-made . . .
by a contractor.

**Yo' Mama's so fat,**

her senior high school picture is an aerial photograph.

**Yo' Mama's so fat,**

her diaphragms come in a Domino's pizza box.

**Yo' Mama's so fat,**

when she goes to the beach, she's the only one who gets a tan.

**Yo' Mama's so fat,**

the moon revolves around her.

**Yo' Mama's so fat,**
she uses a roll of Bounty and a rope for a
tampon.

**Yo' Mama's so fat,**
you can slap her on the hip and ride the
ripples.

**Yo' Mama's so fat,**
maternity clothes look like Barbie clothes
to her.

**Yo' Mama's so fat,**
when your father mounts her, his ears pop.

**Yo' Mama's so fat,**
she said she wants to get into shape, but I
think she's the perfect shape . . . a sphere.

**Yo' Mama's so fat,**
she once stepped on a quarter and made
George Washington cry.

**Yo' Mama's so fat,**
she eats off a satellite dish.

**Yo' Mama's so fat,**
it takes her eighteen hours to put on her
eighteen-hour bra.

**Yo' Mama's so fat,**
at parties, she takes her tits out and makes balloon animals out of them.

**Yo' Mama's so fat,**
after I'm done making love to her, I roll over twice and I'm still on her.

**Yo' Mama's so fat,**
when she was a kid, her daddy made her come inside when it was raining so the grass could get wet.

**Yo' Mama's so fat,**
one day I showed her a picture of her own feet, and she couldn't identify them.

**Yo' Mama's so fat,**
her bra is used for bungee jumping.

**Yo' Mama's so fat,**
she washes her clothes in a swimming pool.

**Yo' Mama's so fat,**
she makes a Sumo wrestler look anorexic.

**Yo' Mama's so fat,**
PLACE YOUR AD HERE is printed on each of her butt cheeks.

### Yo' Mama's so fat,
she needs to gain just ten more pounds to be declared the fifty-first state.

### Yo' Mama's so fat,
she's six feet tall from side to side.

### Yo' Mama's so fat,
she gets out of bed . . . in sections.

### Yo' Mama's so fat,
if she sat down she'd suffocate.

### Yo' Mama's so fat,
when she tries to run, her butt jiggles like Jell-O.

**Yo' Mama's so fat,**
tailors have to run relay races around her to measure her waistline.

**Yo' Mama's so fat,**
she buys her clothes at Umungus R Us.

**Yo' Mama's so fat,**
I had to take a plane, two buses and a cab—just to get to her good side.

**Yo' Mama's so fat,**
when she sits on one side of the house, the foundation pops up.

**Yo' Mama's so fat,**
she has more wrinkles than a Laundromat.

**Yo' Mama's so fat,**
when she got married and yo' father
carried her across the threshold, he had
to make two trips.

**Yo' Mama's so fat,**
yo' father needs a ladder to climb on top of
her whenever they make love.

**Yo' Mama's so fat,**
when she goes to the movies, she sits next to
everybody.

**Yo' Mama's so fat,**
she put a teaspoon of water in the bathtub
and it overflowed when she got in.

**Yo' Mama's so fat,**
when she was born, her mama didn't have a
C-section, she had a C-D-E-F-G section.

**Yo' Mama's so fat,**
she makes King Kong look like a baby chimp.

**Yo' Mama's so fat,**
she put on a Malcolm X shirt and a helicopter
tried to land on her.

### Yo' Mama's so fat,

when she visited SeaWorld Shamu tried to have sex with her.

### Yo' Mama's armpits are so big,

she applies deodorant with a paint roller.

### Yo' Mama's so fat,

all the restaurants in town have signs that say MAXIMUM OCCUPANCY 240 PATRONS OR YO' MAMA.

### Yo' Mama's so fat,

she showers at the car wash.

**Yo' Mama's so fat,**
when she goes to the beach, Greenpeace
comes to save her.

**Yo' Mama's so fat,**
when she was bad as a child, her father made
her stand in all four corners.

**Yo' Mama's so fat,**
a map of the world could fit on a pimple on
her ass.

**Yo' Mama's so fat,**
every time she wears a gray suit, an admiral
tries to board her.

**Yo' Mama's so fat,**
she uses a car tire as a headband.

**Yo' Mama's so fat,**
you need a map and compass to find your
way around her.

**Yo' Mama's so fat,**
after sex she smokes ham.

**Yo' Mama's so fat,**
she took her dress to the cleaners and they
told her, "Sorry, we don't do drapes."

**Yo' Mama's so fat,**
when her thighs rub together it sounds like corduroy.

**Yo' Mama's so fat,**
she has to be greased before she can walk through the door.

**Yo' Mama's so fat,**
at Christmas the kids hang ornaments on her chins.

**Yo' Mama's so fat,**
she had a real train haul her caboose down the aisle at her wedding.

### Yo' Mama's so ugly,

farmers pay top dollar for her to stand in the fields and scare the crows away.

### Yo' Mama's so ugly,

she's a living example of why some animals eat their young.

### Yo' Mama's so ugly,

she has to sneak up on tomorrow.

### Yo' Mama's so ugly,

when the Church passes the collection basket to help suffering war victims, the Priest always points to yo' Mama as an example.

**Yo' Mama's so ugly,**

she could be a poster child for the burn center.

**Yo' Mama's so ugly,**

your father took up drinking right after the operation he had that restored his eyesight.

**Yo' Mama's so ugly,**

she could make k. d. lang go straight.

**Yo' Mama's so ugly,**

even her Rice Krispies won't talk to her.

**Yo' Mama's so ugly,**
yo' father put the bathroom mirror inside the medicine cabinet.

**Yo' Mama's so ugly,**
you can't tell which parent is which.

**Yo' Mama's so ugly,**
when she was a child she had to trick or treat over the telephone.

**Yo' Mama's so ugly,**
your father has to spray himself with Mace right before having sex with her.

### Yo' Mama's so ugly,
the Elephant Man calls her an animal.

### Yo' Mama's so ugly,
she looks like the last shit I took.

### Yo' Mama's so ugly,
she makes Tammy Faye Baker look like a
*Cosmopolitan* cover model.

### Yo' Mama's so ugly,
when she was a child, her parents sent her to
the movies—then moved.

### Yo' Mama's so ugly,

when she was a child her father tied a bone around her neck so the puppies would play with her.

### Yo' Mama's so ugly,

you should paint two eyes and a nose on her crotch and get her to walk on her hands.

### Yo' Mama's so ugly,

your father has pet names for all those hairy warts on her face.

**Yo' Mama's so ugly,**
her own shadow is afraid of her.

**Yo' Mama's so ugly,**
if I was alone in a jungle with her, I'd rather
screw a baboon.

**Yo' Mama's so ugly,**
the town took up a collection to help buy
you a brand-new mama.

**Yo' Mama's so ugly,**
The last time she went to the top of the
Empire State Building, she was attacked
by planes.

### Yo' Mama's so ugly,

when friends come to visit her, they wear monster masks to help her feel at home.

### Yo' Mama's so ugly,

her pillow cries at night.

### Yo' Mama wouldn't be so ugly,

if she would just shave her beard.

### Yo' Mama's so ugly,

even her own reflection runs away when it sees her.

### Yo' Mama's so ugly,
she stamps her face in the cookie dough to make gorilla cookies.

### Yo' Mama's so ugly,
when she cussed as a child, her father made her wash her whole face out with soap.

### Yo' Mama has so many zits,
she could start her own oil company.

### Yo' Mama's so ugly,
when she goes to the Jack-in-the-Box drive-thru, Jack jumps back in the box.

**Yo' Mama's so short,**
she goes swimming in a bottle cap.

**Yo' Mama's so short,**
she uses a cap from a Bic pen as a diaphragm.

**Yo' Mama's so short,**
she scuba dives in the fish bowl.

**Yo' Mama's so short,**
she's not big enough to ride the wheel in a
hamster cage.

**Yo' Mama's so short,**
she looks up to everyone.

**Yo' Mama's so short,**
she takes an elevator to get up to her bed.

**Yo' Mama's so short,**
she buys her clothes at the Barbie section of
the toy store.

**Yo' Mama's so short,**
she has sex with your sister's Ken doll.

**Yo' Mama's so short,**
she has to look up to look down.

**Yo' Mama's so short,**
her crabs are bigger than she is.

**Yo' Mama's so short,**
I could use her as a spitball and shoot her
through my straw.

**Yo' Mama's so short,**
she flies to Miami each year . . . strapped
to a goose.

**Yo' Mama's so short,**
your dog likes to bury her in the woods.

**Yo' Mama's so short,**
she could bungee jump off my shoelaces.

**Yo' Mama's so short,**
she could ride on the back of a roach, and
her legs would still dangle.

**Yo' Mama's so short,**
she tried to commit suicide by jumping off a
curb.

**Yo' Mama's so old,**
she remembers the Alamo.

**Yo' Mama's so old,**
she lived at the Gettysburg address.

**Yo' Mama's so old,**
she knew Ronald McDonald when he was in
clown school.

**Yo' Mama's so old,**
she knew Ivan the Terrible when he was just
mildly annoying.

### YO' MAMA'S SO OLD . . .

**Yo' Mama's so old,**
when the cashier asked for money at the
grocery counter, yo' Mama handed her rocks.

**Yo' Mama's so old,**
she was the caterer for the pilgrims at the
first Thanksgiving dinner.

**Yo' Mama's so old,**
her birthday expired.

**Yo' Mama's so old,**
she still has her Olympic ticket stub . . . from
1100 B.C.

**Yo' Mama's so old,**
when I told her to act her age, she dropped
dead.

**Yo' Mama's so old,**
on her birthday, the candles cost more than
the cake.

**Yo' Mama's so old,**
she remembers turning tricks for a nickel.

**Yo' Mama's so old,**
when she was in school, history was current
events.

**Yo' Mama's so old,**
scientists claim she's the missing link.

**Yo' Mama's so old,**
she shits petrified wood.

**Yo' Mama's so old,**
she swam in the Dead Sea when it was
still alive.

**Yo' Mama's so skinny,**
she uses Chapstick as underarm deodorant.

**Yo' Mama's so skinny,**
she once swallowed a grape and was rushed
to the maternity hospital.

**Yo' Mama's so skinny,**
when she wears a fur coat, she looks like a
pipe cleaner.

**Yo' Mama's so skinny,**
if she turned sideways she'd be invisible.

**Yo' Mama's so skinny,**
when I go down on her, it looks like I'm
playing the flute.

**Yo' Mama's so skinny,**
she could dodge snowflakes.

**Yo' Mama's so skinny,**
she gets lost in between the couch cushions.

**Yo' Mama's so skinny,**
she hula hoops with a Cheerio.

**Yo' Mama's so skinny,**
she can limbo underneath a closed door.

**Yo' Mama's so skinny,**
she uses a Q-Tip as a tampon.

**Yo' Mama's so skinny,**
you have to tie knots in her arms and legs to
make elbows and knees.

### Yo' Mama's so tall,
she hangs her laundry between telephone poles.

### Yo' Mama's so tall,
she's able to leap tall buildings at a single bound.

### Yo' Mama's so tall,
even Wilt Chamberlain has to stand up to go down on her.

**Yo' Mama's so tall,**
planes get caught in her hair net.

**Yo' Mama's so tall,**
on her fifth birthday, her parents gave her
weather balloons.

**Yo' Mama's so tall,**
she needs a telescope to see her feet.

**Yo' Mama's so tall,**
she doesn't understand when people ask her
if she wants to "get high."

**Yo' Mama's so tall,**
her head registers a huge blip on LaGuardia's
radar screens.

**Yo' Mama's so black,**
she has no shadow.

**Yo' Mama's so black,**
when she stands next to a mountain she
looks like a tunnel.

**Yo' Mama's so black,**
people go to sleep whenever she walks outside.

**Yo' Mama's so black,**
when she enters a room, people think there's
a power outage.

MAMAMAMAMAMAMAMAMAMA**57**AMAMAMAMAMAMAMAMA-

**Yo' Mama's so black,**
when she lay down on her bed, yo' father
thought he burned another hole in the mattress.

**Yo' Mama's so black,**
to find her in a room she has to open her
mouth so you can see her teeth.

**Yo' Mama's so black,**
she could show up at a funeral naked.

**Yo' Mama's so black,**
yo' family practices daylight savings time all
year round.

**Yo' Mama's so black,**
she absorbs light.

**Yo' Mama's so black,**
if she were on TV everyone watching would
think the tube was blown.

**Yo' Mama's so white,**
when she walks into a movie theater
everyone yells, "Shut off the lights!"

**Yo' Mama's so white,**
her nickname is Caspar.

**Yo' Mama's so white,**
yo' father took her to a Macy's white sale
and lost her.

**Yo' Mama's so white,**
put a cap on her head and she'll look like a
milk bottle.

**Yo' Mama's so white,**
when she opens her mouth kids dunk
cookies in her.

**Yo' Mama's so white,**
when she has the runs, she shits mashed
potatoes.

**Yo' Mama's so white,**
she's the new mascot for White Cloud
toilet paper.

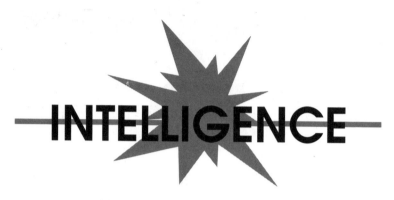

### INTELLIGENCE

**Yo' Mama's so stupid,**
she goes to the library to get a book of matches.

**Yo' Mama's so stupid,**
she thinks Chevy Chase is a funny car race.

**Yo' Mama's so stupid,**
she brings toilet paper to a crap game.

**Yo' Mama's so stupid,**
after she smacked up her car, she went to the
store to buy a tube of Fixadent.

**Yo' Mama's so stupid,**
she thinks Hamburger Helper comes with a
person.

**Yo' Mama's so stupid,**
she thinks Moby Dick is a venereal
disease.

**Yo' Mama's so stupid,**
she thinks an innuendo is an Italian suppository.

**Yo' Mama's so stupid,**
she got run over by a parked car.

**Yo' Mama's so stupid,**
she took the Pepsi challenge, and chose Jif.

**Yo' Mama's so stupid,**
she studies for a Pap test.

**Yo' Mama's so stupid,**
when she went to a movie and it said, "under seventeen not admitted," she went home to find sixteen relatives.

**Yo' Mama's so stupid,**
she sold her car for gas money.

**Yo' Mama's so stupid,**
it takes her two hours to watch 60 Minutes.

**Yo' Mama's so stupid,**
she flunked a sign language class because she
couldn't hear the teacher.

**Yo' Mama's so stupid,**
she was the quality control inspector for the
M&M factory, but got fired for throwing out
the ones with the Ws on them.

### Yo' Mama's so stupid,
she thinks a Henna is an Italian chicken.

### Yo' Mama's so stupid,
she once tripped and fell up a flight of stairs.

### Yo' Mama's so stupid,
she almost froze to death at a drive-in theater
when she went to see a movie called
*Closed for the Winter.*

### Yo' Mama's so shallow,
you could rent space in her head.

## YO' MAMA'S SO STUPID . . .

**Yo' Mama's so stupid,**
she snuck out of a nudist colony to see what she'd look like in a bathing suit.

**Yo' Mama's so stupid,**
she's a prime example of what happens when two cousins engage in sex.

**Yo' Mama's so stupid,**
she tripped over a cordless phone.

**Yo' Mama's so stupid,**
she thinks Forrest Gump is a grouchy hermit who lives in Central Park.

**Yo' Mama's so stupid,**
she thinks menopause is a five-minute
intermission at a Mel Gibson movie.

**Yo' Mama's so stupid,**
she thinks Peter Pan is the wash basin in the
men's room.

**Yo' Mama's so stupid,**
she thinks apartheid means to spread her legs.

**Yo' Mama's so stupid,**
she's still looking for the Kraft Singles bar.

**Yo' Mama's so stupid,**
she thinks lobotomy is a new dance craze.

**Yo' Mama's so stupid,**
she cooks with Old Spice.

**Yo' Mama's so stupid,**
your father asked her to buy a color TV but
she didn't know which color to get.

**Yo' Mama's so stupid,**
she thinks the crash test dummies die every
time they have a wreck.

**Yo' Mama's so stupid,**
she planted the money tree her sister gave her
for Christmas.

**Yo' Mama's so stupid,**
she brought a rabbit to a hair salon.

**Yo' Mama's so stupid,**
she went to the lost and found and asked if
they had her virginity.

**Yo' Mama's so stupid,**
she thinks Fellatio is an Italian Opera.

**Yo' Mama's so stupid,**
she thinks the Minute Men in the American
Revolution were rice pickers.

**Yo' Mama's so stupid,**
she thinks daylight savings time is an annual
sale at Macy's.

**Yo' Mama's so stupid,**
she thought a quarterback was a refund.

**Yo' Mama's so stupid,**
she thinks she can get Lyme disease
from Tic Tacs.

**Yo' Mama's so stupid,**
she thinks that a pawn shop is a
chess players' club.

**Yo' Mama's so stupid,**
she thinks tofu is a guy with a foot fetish.

**Yo' Mama's so stupid,**
she went to a mind reader and was only
charged half price.

**Yo' Mama's so stupid,**
when yo' father asked her what she thought
about Red China, she said "Fine, so long as it
doesn't clash with the tablecloth."

**Yo' Mama's so stupid,**
she thinks Johnny Cash is a pay toilet.

**Yo' Mama's so stupid,**
she thinks Ping Pong balls are a Chinese
venereal disease.

**Yo' Mama's so stupid,**
she thinks the Kentucky Derby is a hat.

**Yo' Mama's so stupid,**
she has to take her shoes off to count to twenty.

**Yo' Mama's so stupid,**
she brought cosmetics to a make-up exam.

### Yo' Mama's so slow,

she went to the grocery store to get your baby sister's formula, but by the time she got back, your sister moved out, got married, and had two kids of her own.

### Yo' Mama's so slow,

if she walked any slower she'd go backwards.

### Yo' Mama's so slow,

she walks like a snail with hemorrhoids.

**Yo' Mama's so slow,**
she begins cooking Christmas dinner in July.


**Yo' Mama's so slow,**
by the time she climbs the corporate ladder,
the steps will have rotted.

# PERSONALITY

**Yo' Mama's so messed up,**
the last mosquito that bit her got arrested
for DWI.

**Yo' Mama's so schitzo,**
she has a personality for every day of the week.

**Yo' Mama's so psycho,**
even the lice in her hair are on Prozac.

**Yo' Mama has so many personalities,**
the landlord wants to raise the rent $50 for
each of them.

**Yo' Mama's so messed up,**
she can't remember whether or not drinking
affects her memory.

**Yo' Mama's so messed up,**
during a cab ride, she asked the driver if there
was room in the car for a pizza and a six pack . . .
the driver said yes, so she threw up.

**Yo' Mama's so messed up,**
the only difference between her and a
terrorist—the terrorist makes fewer demands.

**Yo' Mama's so messed up,**
she tried to write a song about alcohol, but
she never made it past the first few bars.

**Yo' Mama's such a lush,**
miners use her mouth as a torch.

**Yo' Mama's such a lush,**
even Johnny Walker runs from her.

**Yo' Mama's so cold,**
her asshole could double as a frozen yogurt
machine.

**Yo' Mama's so cold,**
her crabs keep fresh for weeks.

**Yo' Mama's so cold,**
the only time she has a heart is when she
plays poker.

**Yo' Mama's so cold,**
the last time I slept with her, I got frostbite.

**Yo' Mama's so cold,**
during the last blizzard yo' father slept
outside 'cause it was warmer.

**Yo' Mama's so cold,**
yo' father had to take out a loan to pay the
heating bill . . . in July.

# HYGIENE

**Yo' Mama's so stench,**
the military wants to harness her farts for
chemical warfare.

**Yo' Mama's so stench,**
nine out of ten prisoners on death row given
the choice of the electric chair or a day in a
room alone with yo' Mama choose the chair.

**Yo' Mama's so stench,**
she produces more gas than Exxon.

**Yo' Mama's so stench,**
your father rolls deodorant on her whole
body when she's sleeping.

**Yo' Mama's so stench,**
the word "radioactive" is tattooed on her butt.

**Yo' Mama's so stench,**
she sweats Black Flag.

**Yo' Mama's so stench,**
her underwear reads ENTER AT YOUR OWN RISK.

**Yo' Mama's so stench,**
when she calls information, the operator
passes out.

**Yo' Mama's so dirty,**
her aura is black.

**Yo' Mama's so dirty,**
she gets ringworm around the collar.

**Yo' Mama's so dirty,**
kids write "wash me" on her back
with their fingers.

**Yo' Mama's so dirty,**
she needs a weed wacker to cut her hair.

**Yo' Mama's so dirty,**
animals lick food stains off her shirt.

**Yo' Mama's so dirty,**
farmers use her body to grow mushrooms.

**Yo' Mama's so dirty,**
she has to wash behind her ears with a
power hose.

# SEXUALITY

**Yo' Mama's so loose,**
she's like subway tracks—under everything
that moves and laid all over the city.

**Yo' Mama's so loose,**
yo' father's gotta tie one end of a rope around
his waist and the other around the bedpost
when they do the nasty.

**Yo' Mama's so loose,**
her gynecologist needs a floodlight
to examine her.

**Yo' Mama's so loose,**
there's stalactites growing on the roof
of her uterus.

**If sluttiness were blades of grass,**
yo' Mama would be the White House lawn.

**Yo' Mama's so loose,**
her G-string says "eat at the Y."

**Yo' Mama's such a slut,**
she's known as the "Have It Your Way Girl" at Burger King.

**Yo' Mama's such a ho',**
they call her Norelco . . . home of the triple head.

**Yo' Mama's such a ho',**
she holds her own red-light specials.

**Yo' Mama's so loose,**
yo' father puts on diving gear before having sex with her.

**Yo' Mama's so loose,**
even Santa calls her a Ho-Ho-Ho.

**Yo' Mama's like**
a television; even a child could turn her on.

**Yo' Mama's so loose,**
she walks around town with a mattress
strapped to her back.

**Yo' Mama's so loose,**
she wears a dollar on her belt and a sign that
says ALL YOU CAN EAT FOR UNDER A BUCK.

**Yo' Mama's so loose,**
she's like the Energizer Bunny, she keeps
going and going and going and going . . .

**Yo' Mama's so loose,**
she's like a bowling ball—first you finger
her, then you throw her in the gutter.

**Yo' Mama's like**
a vacuum cleaner—she sucks, blows, and
gets laid in the closet.

**Yo' Mama's so loose,**
she has a tattoo of a man holding a ruler
saying, YOU MUST BE THIS BIG TO ENTER THE RIDE.

**Yo' Mama's so loose,**
she's like butter—she spreads for bread.

**Yo' Mama's so loose,**
she's like a turtle—once she's on her back,
she's screwed.

**Yo' Mama's like**
an elevator—you push her button and she'll
go down.

**Yo' Mama's so loose,**
her idea of safe sex is putting the car in park.

# SOCIAL STATUS

**Yo' Mama's so poor,**
even the pot she's got to piss in has a hole in it.

**Yo' Mama's so poor,**
she serves her party guests Listerine as cocktails.

**Yo' Mama's so poor,**
at suppertime she butters the corns on her feet.

**Yo' Mama's so poor,**
she shoplifts at Goodwill.

**Yo' Mama's so poor,**
when your sister asked for a teddy bear last Christmas, yo' Mama gave her a fur ball that the cat coughed up.

**Yo' Mama's so poor,**
when you cried to yo' Mama for food, she said, "Shut up—I fed you last week."

**Yo' Mama's so poor,**
when I moved some newspaper to sit down on the couch, yo' Mama said, "Who took off the sofa cover?"

**Yo' Mama's house is so poor,**
the dog begs the roaches for scraps.

**Yo' Mama's so poor,**
she couldn't afford a piñata for a Mexican
fiesta, so she hung up a pregnant dog.

**Yo' Mama's so poor,**
she goes bar-hopping for the pretzels.

**Yo' Mama's so poor,**
whenever she gets hungry, she just brings
home a new animal from the A.S.P.C.A.

# BODY PARTS

**Yo' Mama's nose is so big,**
she could smell people farting in Poland.

**Yo' Mama's nose is so big,**
birds sometimes get sucked in.

**Yo' Mama's nose is so big,**
she could inhale Colombia with one snort.

**Yo' Mama's nose is so big,**
she practices giving head with it.

**Yo' Mama's nose is so big,**
she uses queen-sized bedsheets as tissues.

**Yo' Mama's nose is so big,**
squirrels use it to store their nuts.

**Yo' Mama's nose hairs are so long,**
I could double Dutch with them.

**Yo' Mama's nose is so big,**
you could pitch a tent inside of it.

**Yo' Mama's nose is so big,**
while walking in New York, she caught a cold
in California.

**Yo' Mama's armpits are so hairy,**
it looks like she has Don King in a headlock.

**Yo' Mama's so hairy,**
she's the understudy for Cousin Itt.

**Yo' Mama's so hairy,**
you could wrap her chest hairs in a French
braid.

**Yo' Mama's so bald,**
when she was a baby, her mama used to
powder the wrong end.

**Yo' Mama's so bald,**
it looks like she's wearing a diaphragm on her head.

**Yo' Mama's so bald,**
her lice surrendered.

**Yo' Mama's so bald**
and wrinkled, her face looks like a nipple.

**Yo' Mama's so bald,**
her nickname is Spalding.

**Yo' Mama's so bald,**
when she takes a shower, she gets brainwashed.

**Yo' Mama's so cross-eyed,**
she once dropped a dime and picked up two nickels.

**Yo' Mama's glasses are so thick,**
when she looks down a pothole, she sees Hell.

**Yo' Mama's so cross-eyed,**
when she's havin' sex with yo' father, she
thinks it's an orgy.

**Yo' Mama's so blind,**
she has spare glasses so she can find her
glasses when she loses them.

### Yo' Mama's so near-sighted,

her car mirrors say OBJECTS ARE JUST ABOUT TO SMASH YO' ASS.

### Yo' Mama's so blind,

she played one of three mice in her nursery school play.

### Yo' Mama's so near-sighted,

she wears binoculars strapped to her face to read a book.

### Yo' Mama's so cross-eyed,

she chews quadruplemint gum.

**Yo' Mama's ears are so large,**
she's starting her own wax company.

**Yo' Mama's ears are so large,**
the New York Yankees offered her a contract
to catch fly balls in centerfield.

**Yo' Mama's ears are so large,**
she uses them to slap you while her hands
are busy cooking.

**Yo' Mama's ears are so large,**
she could hear people flipping her the bird.

**Yo' Mama's ears are so large,**
she uses palm trees as Q-Tips.

**Yo' Mama's ears are so large,**
she could tell secrets to herself.

**Yo' Mama's ears are so large,**
she uses them to play peek-a-boo.

**Yo' Mama's ears are so large,**
she could stick her elbows in them.

**Yo' Mama's ears are so large,**
corn farmers are jealous.

**Yo' Mama's ears are so large,**
when she goes to a restaurant, people hang
their coats on them.

**Yo' Mama's mouth is so big,**
she could swallow a banana sideways.

**Yo' Mama's lips are so big,**
she could French kiss a moose.

**Yo' Mama's lips are so big,**
you could wet them and stick her to the wall.

**Yo' Mama's lips are so big,**
she could wax cars with them.

**Yo' Mama's lips are so big,**
she could blow an entire football team at the
same time.

## YO' MAMA'S MOUTH . . .

**Yo' Mama's lips are so big,**
she could kiss her own face.

**Yo' Mama's lips are so big,**
she has to spray her lipstick on.

**Yo' Mama's lips are so big,**
she could kiss my ass, your ass, and still have
room for some more heinie.

**Yo' Mama's lips are so big,**
Chapstick had to make a spray.

**Yo' Mama's so bucktoothed,**
she could kiss your father on the cheek and
comb his beard at the same time.

**Yo' Mama has one tooth**
and she uses it to chop wood.

**Yo' Mama has one tooth**
and she uses it to punch holes in bagels.

**Yo' Mama's so toothless,**
when she smiles her mouth looks like an
ear of Indian corn.

**Yo' Mama's so bucktoothed,**
when I French kissed her she removed my
tonsils.

**Yo' Mama's so bucktoothed,**
when she smiles, it looks like the Olympic ski
jump.

**Yo' Mama's so bucktoothed,**
you could show movies on them.

**Yo' Mama's so bucktoothed,**
Del Monte hired her to remove corn from the
cobs.

## YO' MAMA'S BREASTS . . .

**Yo' Mama's tits are so small,**
your father took her to a tire shop because
the sign read WE FIX FLATS.

**Yo' Mama's so flat,**
carpenters use her as a level.

**Yo' Mama's tits are so big,**
they're in separate time zones.

**Yo' Mama's tits are so big,**
Sally Struthers wants to harness them to feed
the children.

**Yo' Mama's tits are so big,**
photos of missing children are printed on the
sides of them.

**Yo' Mama's tits are so big,**
they're inspected each month by the FDA.

**Yo' Mama's tits are so small,**
her bras are strapless and cupless.

**Yo' Mama's tits are so big,**
at Christmas time, she hangs her bras over
the fireplace because they hold more stuff.

**Yo' Mama's tits are so big,**
someone tried to serve one in a volleyball
game.

**Yo' Mama's feet are so big,**
she uses two eighteen-wheelers for roller
skates.

**Yo' Mama's feet are so big,**
she has to buy shoes for each toe.

**Yo' Mama's feet are so small,**
when she walks on the sidewalk, she gets
stuck in the cracks.

**Yo' Mama's feet are so big,**
Al Bundy gets a bonus every time he sells her
a pair of shoes.

**Yo' Mama's shoes are so old,**
when she took them off, her feet
disintegrated.

**Yo' Mama's feet are so big,**
she needs a tire gauge to check her Reebok
pumps.

**Yo' Mama's feet are so big,**
Smokey the Bear hired her to stamp out
forest fires.

**Yo' Mama's feet are so huge,**
it takes two cows to make yo' Mama one pair
of sandals.

**Yo' Mama's shoes are so old,**
when she steps in shit, shit gets embarrassed.

# HOW TO MAKE YO' OWN YO' MAMAS

It's really easy to make yo' own Yo' Mama insults. If you choose to make them ahead of time, you'll be well-prepared to do Dozens battle. If you choose to be spontaneous, it's a little harder, but a quick mind that can do it always has the edge in a match. Follow these three easy steps and you'll be bustin' like the best of 'em:

1. Pick a characteristic category (either "physical" or "mental"—these two cover just about everything).

2. Now pick a topic under that category. If "physical," you could pick "fat," "bald" "ugly," etc. If "mental," you could try "stupid," "slow," "cold," "messed up," "loose," etc.

3. Then use one or both of these techniques:

*Association Method:* Remember all that stuff about similes in English class? Now there's finally a practical use for them. A simile is when something is "like" something else (e.g., Yo' Mama's like the subway tracks—she gets laid all over the city). When making Yo' Mama busts, try to think of what people, places, and things are like the topic you're using. For example, if we're busting on "fat," think of things that you know are huge (e.g., whales, states, billboards), heavy (e.g., cargo), obscuring (e.g., trees, eclipses), and use them for the basis of yo' busts.

*Situation Method:* The other way of coming up with original Yo' Mama insults is to look at situations and how Yo' Mama being a certain way (such as fat, stupid, etc.) would affect what happens or what special treatment Yo' Mama would have to get if she was *sooooo* fat or *sooooo* stupid, etc.

Take normal things that you or people around you do. How about yearbook pictures? How would they be taken if Yo' Mama was *sooooo* fat? From an airplane perhaps. Or, think about what kind of an effect Yo' Mama would have on things around her because of her condition. If she was *sooooo* fat, she might trigger an earthquake when she walks in Los Angeles. She might be *sooooo* fat that when she walks (something normal) the records skip at the radio station miles away.

If you're doing a topic such as "stupid," think of things that are *sooooo* easy to do and, of course, make Yo' Mama totally inept at doing it (e.g., Yo' Mama's so stupid, she had a job at the M&M factory, but got fired for throwing away all of the ones with the Ws.) Also try plays on words and pronunciations. An "innuendo" could sound like an Italian suppository to someone who never heard of the word or "Southside Johnny" a toilet across town. See all the possibilities?

# WINNING YO' MAMA STRATEGIES

Whether you use Yo' Mama busts from our book, your memory, or from working with one of the Yo' Mama development techniques, the first and most important thing to remember if you want to consistently win at the Dozens is to know your *opponent*. If someone challenges you on the spot, try to set a time and place for it if you can without losing face. You'll have time to prepare.

Take a good hard look at your opponent. Figure out what the most sensitive areas are and try to rile. For example, if their mama really is fat, you can use mostly fat busts.

Oftentimes, you can size up your opponent and figure out what his/her weak areas are without even considering Mama. Remember, most Yo' Mamas are just a projection of how you feel about the person you're busting on. So, if your opponent is having a hard time in school, stupid snaps might be most effective. If your opponent is really short, try short cuts. And, most crowds will tend to rate those direct insults higher when they can visually verify it with your opponent.

# YO! WE'LL MAKE YOU FAMOUS

## Yo' Own Yo' Mamas Submission Form

Andy Warhol once said that everyone is famous for at least 15 minutes in his lifetime. Here's yo' big chance at fame! Use the form on the next page to send us your ORIGINAL Yo' Mama. If we use it in our next book, *Mo' o' Yo' Mama*, we'll put your name by it and you'll go down in history. AND, we'll send a free copy of the book to the authors of the first 100 original Yo' Mama busts that we use, so don't hesitate!

## SUBMISSION FORM

Cut here or copy this form on an 8½" x 11" piece of paper.

Name: _____

Address: _____

Bust: _____

_____

_____

Send to: Yo' Mama P.O. Box    P.O. Box 127, Stony Point, NY 10980

*I hereby declare that the above quote ("Quote") is of my own original author-ship and agree to allow the authors to use it in the upcoming book, Mo' o' Yo' Mama, and for any other purpose that they see fit at their discretion, so long as the authors identify its source as myself if published in Mo' o' Yo' Mama.*

Print Name _____ Date _____

Signature (if 18 years or older)_____

Parent or Guardian Name (if under 18 years)_____

Parent or Guardian Signature (if under 18 years) _____